SKYE

A LANDSCAPE FASHIONED BY GEOLOGY

SCOTTISH NATURAL HERITAGE

Scottish Natural Heritage 2000
ISBN 1 85397 026 3
A CIP record is held at the British Library

Acknowledgements
Authors: David Stephenson, Jon Merritt, BGS
Series editor: Alan McKirdy, SNH.

Photography
BGS 7, 8 bottom, 10 top left, 10 bottom right, 15 right, 17 top right,19 bottom right, **C.H. Emeleus** 12
bottom, **L. Gill/SNH** 4, 6 bottom, 11 bottom, 12 top left, 18, **J.G. Hudson** 9 top left, 9 top right, back
cover **P&A Macdonald** 12 top right, **A.A. McMillan** 14 middle, 15 left, 19 bottom left, **J.W.Merritt** 6
top, 11 top, 16, 17 top left, 17 bottom, 17 middle, 19 top, **S. Robertson** 8 top, **I. Sarjeant** 9 bottom,
D.Stephenson front cover, 5, 14 top, 14 bottom.

Photographs by Photographic Unit, BGS Edinburgh may be purchased from Murchison House.
Diagrams and other information on glacial and post-glacial features are reproduced from
published work by **C.K. Ballantyne** (p18), **D.I. Benn** (p16), **J.J. Lowe** and **M.J.C. Walker**.

Further copies of this booklet and other publications can be obtained from:
The Publications Section,
Scottish Natural Heritage,
Battleby, Redgorton,
Perth PH1 3EW
Tel: 01783 444177 Fax: 01783 827411

Cover image:
Pinnacle Ridge, Sgurr Nan Gillean, Cullin; gabbro carved by glaciers.

Back page image:
Cannonball concretions in Mid Jurassic age sandstone, Valtos.

SKYE

A Landscape Fashioned by Geology

by

David Stephenson and Jon Merritt

Trotternish from the south; trap landscape due to lavas dipping gently to the west

Contents

If you ask any visitor what attracts them to Skye, all will probably mention the scenery - that magical combination of landscape, vegetation and land use which makes Skye unique in the British Isles, or indeed Europe. In this booklet we aim to show how all these factors have been influenced by the geology - the rocks, the sediments and landforms created by a wide variety of natural processes over many millions of years.

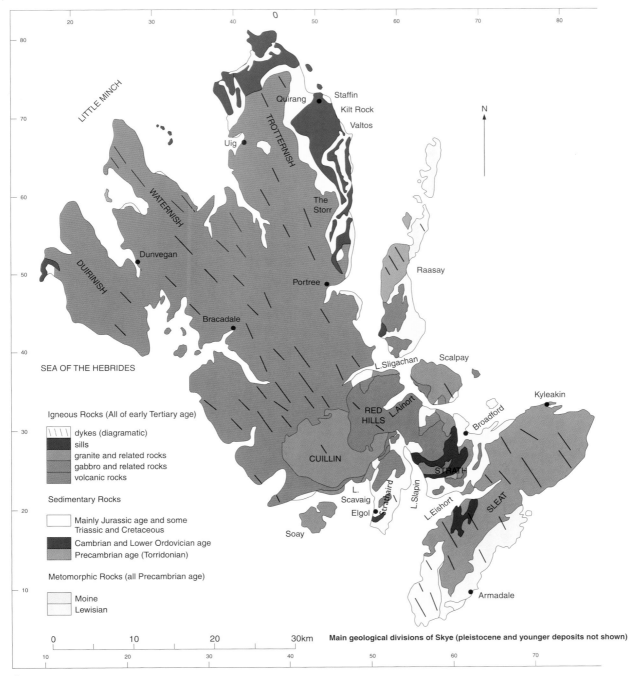

Main geological divisions of Skye (pleistocene and younger deposits not shown)

LITTLE MINCH

TROTTERNISH

Quirang
Staffin
Kilt Rock
Valtos

Uig

The Storr

WATERNISH

Raasay

DUIRNISH

Dunvegan

Portree

SEA OF THE HEBRIDES

Bracadale

L.Sligachan

Scalpay

Kyleakin

RED HILLS

L.Ainort

Broadford

CUILLIN

STRATH

L. Scavaig

Strathaird

L.Slapin

L.Eishort

SLEAT

Elgol

Soay

Armadale

Igneous Rocks (All of early Tertiary age)

dykes (diagramatic)
sills
granite and related rocks
gabbro and related rocks
volcanic rocks

Sedimentary Rocks

Mainly Jurassic age and some
Triassic and Cretaceous
Cambrian and Lower Ordovician age
Precambrian age (Torridonian)

Metomorphic Rocks (all Precambrian age)

Moine
Lewisian

0   10   20   30km

10   20   30   40

N

Setting the Scene

Since the early nineteenth century, professional and amateur geologists alike have been inspired by the spectacular landforms, geological structures, rocks, minerals and fossils of Skye. Generations of students have learned their practical geology here and many fundamental theories of worldwide significance have been developed and tested.

The oldest rocks on Skye are found on the Sleat Peninsula. These Lewisian gneisses are also some of the oldest in Europe. They were formed around 2,800 million years ago from a wide variety of even older rocks which were modified by the effects of heat and intense pressure deep in the earth's crust.

By about 1,100 million years ago, these Lewisian rocks had been raised to the surface of the earth by powerful earth movements and had been worn away by wind and water to form a hummocky land surface. This surface was then gradually buried beneath several thousand metres of gritty and pebbly sandstones, known as the Torridonian - the products of fast-flowing rivers which swept across an otherwise hot, dry landscape.

At this time, the Lewisian gneisses and their Torridonian cover were part of a huge continent, the remains of which now form large parts of Canada and Greenland. North-western Scotland lay on the south-eastern margin of this continent which, by 550 million years ago, had been eroded to a gentle, low-lying landscape bordered by a broad, shallow continental shelf. Beneath its tranquil seas, a sequence of sands, silts and limy muds were laid down during the Cambrian and Ordovician periods.

At the same time, far to the south-east, dramatic earth movements were afoot.

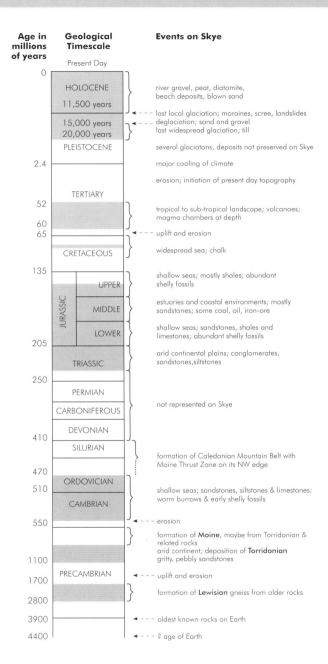

Age in millions of years	Geological Timescale	Events on Skye
	Present Day	
0	HOLOCENE	river gravel, peat, diatomite, beach deposits, blown sand
	11,500 years	
	15,000 years	last local glaciation; moraines, scree, landslides; deglaciation; sand and gravel
	20,000 years	last widespread glaciation; till
	PLEISTOCENE	several glaciatons, deposits not preserved on Skye
2.4		major cooling of climate
	TERTIARY	erosion; initiation of present day topography
52		tropical to sub-tropical landscape; volcanoes; magma chambers at depth
60		
65		uplift and erosion
	CRETACEOUS	widespread sea; chalk
135		shallow seas; mostly shales; abundant shelly fossils
	JURASSIC — UPPER	
	JURASSIC — MIDDLE	estuaries and coastal environments; mostly sandstones; some coal, oil, iron-ore
	JURASSIC — LOWER	shallow seas; sandstones, shales and limestones; abundant shelly fossils
205		arid continental plains; conglomerates, sandstones, siltstones
	TRIASSIC	
250		
	PERMIAN	
	CARBONIFEROUS	not represented on Skye
	DEVONIAN	
410		
	SILURIAN	formation of Caledonian Mountain Belt with Moine Thrust Zone on its NW edge
470		
510	ORDOVICIAN	shallow seas; sandstones, siltstones & limestones; worm burrows & early shelly fossils
	CAMBRIAN	
550		erosion
		formation of **Moine**, maybe from Torridonian & related rocks
1100		arid continent; deposition of **Torridonian** gritty, pebbly sandstones
1700	PRECAMBRIAN	uplift and erosion
2800		formation of **Lewisian** gneiss from older rocks
3900		oldest known rocks on Earth
4400		? age of Earth

These movements caused intense folding, alteration by heat and pressure, and even melting. The resultant metamorphic and igneous rocks were lifted up (between 470 and 400 million years ago) to form the Caledonian Mountain Belt whose roots now constitute the bulk of the mainland Scottish Highlands. In scale this was probably similar to the present-day Alps and extended from the Appalachians, through Ireland, northern Britain, and Norway. The north-western limit of these effects passes through the Sleat Peninsula, where the Lewisian gneisses, the Torridonian sandstones, and a group of metamorphosed sandstones from the south-east called the Moine have all been sliced up and folded by the earth movements.

Over the next 200 million years, there is no record of any geological events on Skye. Any rocks which may have been deposited during this time have either been removed by erosion or covered by younger rocks. It is in the Triassic Period, some 250 million years ago, that the record resumes.

By this time, Skye was part of a hot, dry desert area in which silts, sands, and gravel were deposited periodically on wide floodplains. By the beginning of the Jurassic Period, this continental area had been eroded to a low-lying plain, the sea began to encroach and sands and mud were laid down on a shallow marine shelf.

The warm seas teemed with life, and the resulting sedimentary rocks are the most fossil-rich in the Hebrides.

Subsequently, the land surfaces stayed very close to sea level, so that sediments were deposited in estuaries, deltas, mudflats and lagoons, which ranged from freshwater to brackish or, more rarely, marine. The climate was tropical, and coal-forming coastal swamps developed from time to time.

At the end of the Jurassic Period, the sea once again crept across the area, depositing a thick layer of mud.

Another gap in the record follows - from about 140 million to 95 million years ago when, later in the Cretaceous Period, most of the Hebridean area is believed to have been covered by an extensive sea. Widespread deposits of organic oozes, rich in lime, built up on the sea floor. These strata we now recognise as the 'chalk' found mainly in southern and eastern England.

At the beginning of the Tertiary Period, some 65 million years ago, the area of the Hebrides was raised above sea level and most of the rocks of Cretaceous age were eroded away to leave an almost level surface of Jurassic and older rocks. At this time, movements deep inside the earth were beginning to split the earth's crust into huge 'plates', and Greenland began to split away from north-western Europe along the line that is now occupied by the North Atlantic Ocean.

As a consequence of these plate movements, an extensive system of fractures began to develop in the earth's crust. Through these fractures magma welled up and erupted in what was probably the most extensive volcanic episode ever experienced in north-western Europe. The products of these eruptions spread over both sides of the widening North Atlantic. Today they are found in the Inner Hebrides, Northern Ireland, The Rocknall Bank, the Faroes, Jan Mayen Island, Iceland and east Greenland.

The initial outpourings rapidly built up the vast lava plateau of northern Skye. Later activity was more localised and large central volcanoes developed. The volcanic cones and craters have been eroded away, but their roots remain - they form the Cuillin and the Red Hills.

By 52 million years ago, the igneous activity was all over. Sedimentary rocks of Tertiary age are known to have been deposited on top of and, in places, between the lavas, although they are now largely preserved offshore beneath the Sea of the Hebrides. The whole area was then gently stretched and tilted towards the west. This caused faulting, and the faults governed the position of several valleys and the shape of large stretches of the coastline.

For most of the next 50 million years, the area around Skye experienced weathering and erosion in a mostly warm, sub-tropical climate. It was during this long period of erosion that the main elements of Skye's dramatic landscape were developed. The landscape which we see today is determined essentially by the structure and resistance to erosion of the rocks, but there were further - and considerable - modifications of the landforms by glaciers during the Ice Age.

At the beginning of Pleistocene times some 2.4 million years ago, the climate cooled dramatically. Major cycles of climatic fluctuation began. Initially cold episodes, during which mountain corrie glaciers probably first appeared, were separated by shorter warm episodes every 40,000 years or so. The climatic fluctuations, however, became more pronounced about 900,000 years ago. The changes in climate became even more extreme about 450,000 years ago, since when there have been four long, intensely cold, 'glacial' episodes separated by short warm 'interglacials' at roughly 100,000 year intervals. Most of the soils, sediments and weathered rocks which had formed during Tertiary and early Pleistocene time were swept away by ice in the first major widespread glaciation, and it is after this event that Skye probably first became an island.

Coire Lagan; gabbro smoothed and polished by glaciers

During the last widespread glaciation (26,000 to 13,000 years ago), Scotland was covered by an ice-sheet. It enveloped all but the highest pinnacles on Skye and swept away most of the older glacial deposits. Following a sudden climatic warming about 13,300 years ago, the ice cap started to melt. The freshly exposed stony soils were soon colonised by pioneer vegetation such as grasses, sedges, clubmosses, 'alpine' herbs, and dwarf willow. Next came a mosaic of juniper scrub, crowberry, heather, grassland, and birchwood.

Summer temperatures similar to those of today occurred until about 12,000 years ago, when the climate cooled again. By 11,000 years ago, a tundra environment had returned and arctic conditions prevailed.

Investigating climate change; cores have been taken from more than 20 peat bogs on Skye. The painstaking identification of pollen grains and insect remains layer-by-layer in the peat reveal how vegetation and fauna (hence climate) have changed during its slow accumulation since deglaciation of the area. Radiocarbon dates on pieces of wood and peat reveal when the changes occured

Dryas octapetala. This species has survived on the calcareous soils around Torrin since the last glaciation

During a final, relatively short, glaciation 11,000 to 10,000 years ago, corrie glaciers and substantial areas of ice and snow accumulated in the mountains. The surrounding lowland areas were frozen wastes, similar to the conditions found today in parts of arctic Europe and Asia.

Some 10,000 years ago, the climate warmed rapidly. The glaciers melted. The initial pioneer vegetation was soon replaced by birch and hazel woodland, ferns, tall herbs, and scattered willows. Oak and elm arrived on Skye about 9,000 years ago, together with some pine. Alder arrived much later. Mixed birch-hazel-oak woodland flourished until the climate became wetter some 5,200 years ago. At this time, people first began felling trees to plant crops - the beginning of human influence on the landscape.

Grass and heather moorland began to expand at the expense of the woodland, and blanket peat started to accumulate. Pine stumps, regularly found in the peat, are proof of a short-lived expansion of 'Caledonian' pinewood about 4,000 years ago.

As we approach modern times, large areas of woodland survived in the south of the island until about 300 years ago, when cattle grazing became more widespread. As the woods were felled, the human factor became still more telling with increasing use of peat as fuel.

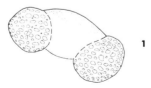

Pollen grains; 1. Pine, 2. Alder, 3. Birch, 4. Spore of Clubmoss, Beetle (5) now found in Siberia

Highly deformed Lewisian gneiss above the Moine Thrust

The Ancient Rocks

Rocks are usually stacked on top of each other in the order in which they were formed, with the oldest at the bottom and the youngest at the top. The rocks of the Sleat Peninsula and adjoining areas of Skye, however, demonstrate that this is not always true. This area is on the north-western edge of what was the Caledonian Mountain Belt. During the formation of this mountain belt, the rocks were tightly folded and overturned so that now they can be right way up or upside down depending on where they are in the folds. On a larger scale, huge sheets of rock several hundred metres thick have been carried many kilometres towards the north-west, sliding over the top of one another so that in general they are now stacked with the oldest on the top. The gently sloping planes of sliding between the transported sheets are known as 'thrusts'. These can be distinguished by zones of very fine-grained rock formed by the intense grinding which took place as the rock masses were moved. The whole terrain affected by these thrusts runs throughout north-west Scotland from Iona in the south to Loch Eriboll in the north and is known as the 'Moine Thrust Zone'.

The Moine Thrust Zone, marking the north-western edge of the Caledonian Mountain Belt, as seen in the Strath area and Sleat. (The vertical scale is greatly exaggerated).

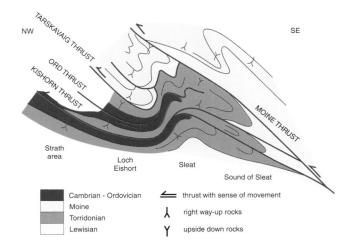

The oldest rocks on Skye, the Lewisian gneisses, occur mainly on the south-east coast of Sleat where they form low, well-rounded rocky hills and produce poor, acid soils. The ancient gneisses are characteristically streaked and banded and any remaining trace of the original rock types have been obliterated by repeated earth movements during their long history. They have been thrust over the top of the younger Torridonian rocks, here predominantly red and brown, gritty and pebbly sandstones, and rocks of the Moine Group, similar to those of the Torridonian but metamorphosed by the heat and pressure of the earth movements. These rocks form the moderately high, heather-clad hills with predominantly terraced slopes. To the north of Loch Eishort, the Torridonian rocks are thrust over the top of still younger rocks of Cambrian to Ordovician age at the north-western edge of the thrust zone.

The Younger Sedimentary Rocks : records of life

0   50
mm

'Pipe rock'; worm burrows in quartzite of Cambrian age

Some of the best agricultural land on Skye is found in the Strath area between Broadford and Loch Slapin. Here the limestones of Cambrian to Ordovician age have created smooth, well-drained, grassy slopes ideal for crofting. Important small shelly fossils have been found in these rocks. These fossils are similar to some of the first hard-shelled organisms to appear worldwide in early Cambrian times. They are, however, very rare and unlikely to be found by the casual visitor. More easily found are the infilled burrows of worm-like organisms which are quite common in parts of the quartzites (hard, very pure sandstones) which lie under the limestone. Some of these burrows are trumpet-shaped and the rocks are commonly known as 'Pipe Rock'.

Much of the area between Broadford and Loch Eishort, the Strathaird Peninsula and the northern and eastern coastal areas of the Trotternish Peninsula consists of sedimentary rocks of Jurassic age. Smaller outcrops occur between Portree and Broadford.

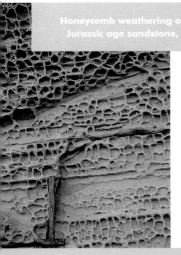

Honeycomb weathering of Mid Jurassic age sandstone, Elgol

Cannonball concretions in Mid Jurassic age sandstone, Valtos

Elgol sea cliffs

Lower Jurassic rocks were deposited mainly in shallow seas and are a varied sequence of limestones, shales and sandstones. On Raasay, this sequence includes the Raasay Ironstone which was mined during the First World War.

Middle Jurassic rocks were deposited mainly in estuaries and are predominantly sandstones with some shales and a few thin limestones. The quartz grains of the sandstones are often cemented together by calcium carbonate which can result in some very strange and fascinating weathering characteristics. At Valtos, for example, the sandstones have been weathered by the elements into large cannonballs which can be up to a metre in diameter. In other places the rocks 'weather-out' in an irregular manner to give a curious 'honeycomb' effect which can be seen in the sea cliffs near Elgol.

Some of the shales from the Jurassic rocks were found to contain up to 17 gallons of crude oil per ton of shale. Although they were never mined commercially onshore, the presence of these oil-rich shales has promoted recent searches for oil in the sea areas off the coast of Skye.

Virtually all of the Jurassic rocks contain fossils. These fossils enable geologists to sub-divide the strata locally and compare them with established Jurassic age successions throughout the world. The limestones and shales are particularly rich in fossils which commonly make up a large part of the rock itself.

9

Typical fossils of Jurassic age from Skye; central ammonite, then clockwise from top left, gastropod, a curved oyster, belemnite, scallop

The most common fossils are different kinds of oysters and other two-shelled organisms, gastropods (sea snails), ammonites (elaborate coiled shells of squid-like creatures), belemnites (like cuttlefish but with a hard, pointed internal shell), crinoids (sea lilies which, despite their name, are actually animals related to sea urchins, and appear to grow from the sea bed like a plant) and corals. Fossils of microscopic organisms are abundant and are particularly helpful to geologists in sub-dividing rock successions. At the other extreme of size are the remains of reptiles such as ichthyosaurs and plesiosaurs - the sea living relatives of the dinosaurs which roamed the land at this time. Fossil plants and indeterminate fragments of fossilised wood show that there was a landmass close by and give an impression of the tropical nature of the vegetation.

A fossilised leaf (Hazel or Beech family) of Tertiary age from sediments between lava flows, Glen Osdale

Gently dipping basalt lavas, looking north from the Quirang

The Lava Plateau

In northern and western Skye the skyline is dominated by the stepped or 'trap' landscape created by lava flows from the volcanoes of Tertiary age which became active around 60 million years ago. These lava flows are horizontal or gently sloping and form distinctive flat-topped hills with stepped sides. The well-known MacLeod's Tables in Duirinish are an excellent example.

Individual lava flows can be up to 10 or 25 metres thick but they are not uniform throughout. At the top and bottom they are usually broken and slaggy with many amygdales (former gas bubbles now filled with minerals). The central parts are usually more solid, some with the distinctive columns which are features of the flows of the Giant's Causeway in Antrim and Fingal's Cave on Staffa. It is this contrast which results in the characteristic stepped landscape.

Accumulations of sedimentary rocks between the lava flows indicate that river systems and lakes were developed between volcanic eruptions, and plant remains within the sediment suggest a sub-tropical or Mediterranean climate. Where a long time elapsed between successive flows, red soils rich in clay developed which are similar to those developing today in wet, tropical or sub-tropical climates.

Junction of lava flows, near Bracadale; note the red layer of rock, formed from a tropical soil, on top of the lower flow

The plateau lavas are mostly basalts and were erupted rapidly, but with little explosive activity, from long cracks in the earth's crust which ran roughly from the north-west to the south-east. Volcanic ash deposits, which indicate more explosive activity, are rarely found, except at the base of the lava pile, which suggests a more dramatic initiation of the Skye volcano.

The Red Hills; granite landscape

The Roots of Volcanoes

The cracks in the earth's surface which fed these volcanic eruptions continued to act as pathways for molten magma long after the surface volcanic activity had ceased. Magma hardened in these fissures as vertical sheets of rock known as 'dykes'. There are many examples of dykes on Skye, particularly on the coast where they cut through the sedimentary rocks and stand proud like walls because they erode less easily than the softer rocks around them.

In northern Skye, the magma also forced its way sideways to form sheets between the layers of sedimentary rocks beneath the lavas. These gently sloping sheets can be up to 90 metres thick and are called 'sills'. Many display well-developed columns throughout most of their thickness. This dramatic effect can be seen in the aptly-named Kilt Rock south of Staffin.

The Cuillin of Skye is acclaimed as the most spectacular mountain range in the British Isles. The arc of jagged peaks, almost 1,000 metres high, which makes up the main Cuillin Ridge, together with Sgurr na Stri and Bla Bheinn are a delight for all visitors, particularly mountaineers. The legendary frictional properties of the rough gabbro and the abundant huge cliffs and slabs, swept clear of debris and polished by glaciation, make this area a playground for rock climbers. Less spectacular but equally attractive in their own way are the Red Hills extending from Glamaig to Beinn na Caillich. The granite of these hills is more uniformly worn by wind and water so that the hills have smooth outlines with few steep rocky faces.

Kilt Rock, Staffin; a sill intruded into sedimentary rocks of Jurassic age

Despite their contrasts, these two groups of hills both represent the deeply eroded roots of large volcanoes. Active volcanoes can be seen in many parts of the world, but if we want to understand how they develop, we must look at long extinct volcanoes such as those of the Inner Hebrides where their roots, exhumed over many millions of years, can be seen. This makes Skye a centre of worldwide recognition and importance.

The mountainous areas that we see now are the solidified remains of the magma chambers which fed the volcanoes. Because they cooled slowly, deep in the earth, they now consist of a wide variety of spectacular and beautiful coarse-grained rocks. In the Cuillin these rocks are almost gabbro - a coarse-grained equivalent of the basalts like those which make up most of the older lava flows which can be seen on Skye. The granites of the Red Hills are the coarse-grained equivalents of other types of lavas which are now largely eroded away.

Scattered around both the Cuillin and the Red Hills are rocks which themselves consist of a jumble of rock fragments of various types, ranging from fine dust particles to huge blocks.

These outcrops are the remains of volcanic "vents" - the pipes through which the magma chambers were connected to highly explosive surface eruptions. The vents contain materials brought up from deeper levels as well as the products of the eruption, such as lava and ash, which have collapsed back down the vent. Good examples of this phenomenon can be seen in the Kilchrist - Kilbride area between Bradford and Torrin.

Magma rising in a gentler, less explosive manner commonly solidifies as fine-grained sheets of rock in contrast to their coarse-grained host rocks. Many of these sheets are vertical dykes and some are near-horizontal sills. In the Cuillin, many take the form of 'cone-sheets' - sloping sheets which have the form of huge cones several kilometres in diameter at the surface, dipping inwards towards the deep centre

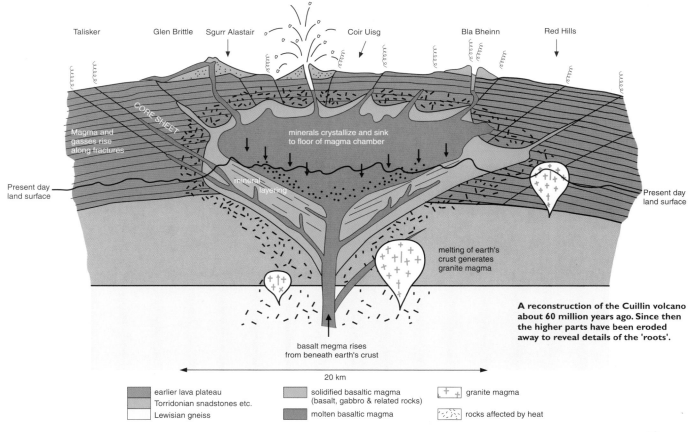

Talisker Glen Brittle Sgurr Alastair Coir Uisg Bla Bheinn Red Hills

CORE SHEET

Magma and gasses rise along fractures

minerals crystallize and sink to floor of magma chamber

Present day land surface

mineral layering

Present day land surface

melting of earth's crust generates granite magma

basalt megma rises from beneath earth's crust

A reconstruction of the Cuillin volcano about 60 million years ago. Since then the higher parts have been eroded away to reveal details of the 'roots'.

20 km

earlier lava plateau
Torridonian snadstones etc.
Lewisian gneiss

solidified basaltic magma (basalt, gabbro & related rocks)
molten basaltic magma

granite magma
rocks affected by heat

of the volcano. The dykes are responsible for much of the jagged outline of the Cuillin mountains because of their different weathering characteristics compared with the surrounding gabbro. They commonly account for notches in the ridge, but can also form upstanding walls or blades like the Inaccessible Pinnacle of Sgurr Dearg. For the climber the sheets often form convenient ledges, but many have a dangerous tendency to brittleness, with many close spaced joints, and are notoriously slippery when wet.

A distinctive feature of the gabbros in some parts of the Cuillin is a very obvious layering reminiscent of that seen in many sedimentary rocks. On closer inspection this is seen to be due to a repetitive variation in the proportions of the individual minerals which make up the rock, such as feldspar, olivine and pyroxene. This happened during the cooling of the magma, as the individual minerals crystallised in a definite order and either floated or sank according to their density relative to the remaining magma. In general the layering dips inwards towards the centre of the magma chamber which consequently has an internal structure resembling a stack of saucers.

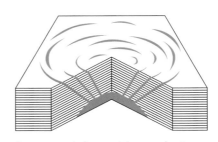

Arrangement of concentric cone-sheets above a magma chamber

Cone-sheets often form convenient ledges

Basalt dyke cutting gabbro, Coire Lagan. The notches in the ridge beyond are caused by the erosion of dykes

Mineral layering in gabbro, Druim Hain

Altered Rocks

mm

Basalt sill cutting altered limestone, Skye Marble Quarry, Torrin

Molten magma of the type which crystallises as basalt or gabbro can be seen as hot as 1200°C. Unlike lava flows, which can cool at the surface within a few days or weeks, large magma chambers at depth stay hot for millions of years, so the effect on the surrounding rocks can be considerable. On Skye, there are a wide variety of older rocks which were very close to the Cuillin and Red Hills magma chambers, and in these areas varying degrees of baking and alteration can be seen in Torridonian sandstones, Cambrian to Ordovician age limestones, Jurassic age sandstones, limestones and shales, and early Tertiary age lavas. It has even been suggested that some of the granite magmas were formed by the melting of Lewisian and Torridonian rocks which lay close to the gabbro magma chambers.

The rocks are not only affected by direct heat. The circulation of heated groundwater and hot fluids expelled from the magma chambers also has played a part in the changes in the rocks.

This alteration can be seen in spectacular form in the Strath area to the south of the Red Hills. Here limestones of Cambrian to Ordovician age have been transformed into the famous Skye marble, quarried near Torrin. The limestone is rich in magnesium and contains nodules of silica - impurities which combine to produce the decorative green and yellow streaks. In places, there are also rare fluorine and boron-bearing minerals. Some rocks, richer in iron, have developed 'magnetite' - the magnetic oxide of iron which was investigated as a potential ore when iron was in great demand during the Second World War.

The Changing Climate and Landscape
Scotland's last glaciations and their effect on Skye

Last widespread glaciation (26,000 - 13,000 years ago)

Evidence from scratch marks (striae), ice-smoothed rocks (roches moutonnées), and rocks carried from their original outcrops by ice (glacial erratics) shows that the mountains of central Skye had their own independent ice cap, while ice from the mainland was diverted both to the north and south of it. The ice swept away the deposits of earlier glaciations, but when it melted, it left behind a widespread undulating sheet of gravelly debris (or 'till') which had been carried along by the ice.

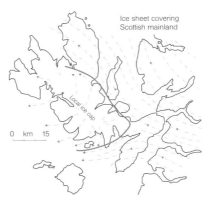

Ice sheet covering
Scottish mainland

Local Ice cap

0   km   15

The last widespread glaciation about 18,000 years ago

The Cuillin Icefield and neighbouring corrie glaciers about 10,500 years ago

16

Perched boulder abandoned by the last glacier in Coir' Uisg

Hummocky moraine as found in Glen Sligachan

Roches mountonnées. Ice moved from left to right

Final Glaciation (11,000 - 10,000 years ago)

Some of the most exciting and exhilarating scenery in Scotland is a result of this final short glaciation. The landforms and sediments caused by it are exceptionally fresh and well-preserved. Terminal moraines at the mouth of Coir' a' Ghrunnda and other corries show that there was a substantial icefield in the Cuillin, with smaller glaciers in the Kyleakin Hills and on the eastern side of the Trotternish Escarpment.

Ice-plucked headwalls and needle-sharp arêtes which formed between neighbouring corrie glaciers now provide extremely challenging climbing. Glaciers reached the sea in lochs Scavaig, Slapin, Sligachan and Ainort, leaving behind widespread hummocky moraines as they retreated. Britain's most impressive screes formed at this time as frost-shattered rocks, formerly supported by the ice that filled the corries, crashed down into the cliffs and gullies. The screes are now largely inactive, but mountainsides continue to be scarred by flash floods, landslides and mud flows during storms. This is particularly clear in the Red Hills, which are strewn with frost-shattered granite rubble.

Coir' Uisg, one of the finest glacially-scoured basins in Britain

Landslides

Landslides of the Quirang, showing the 'Table' in the centre

The landslides of northern Skye are unrivalled in Britain. The best examples fringe the great escarpment of Trotternish where a thick pile of basalt lavas of Tertiary age rests on relatively weak sedimentary rocks of earlier Jurassic age.

With the march of time, the sedimentary rocks gave way to the great weight of the lavas, resulting in enormous landslides and the creation of awesome labyrinths of huge blocks, and pinnacles bearing the evocative names of the Quirang, Table, Needle, Prison, Dùn Dubh and the Old Man of Storr.

The largest and freshest features have formed in the last 13,000 years since the last widespread glaciation, but landslide deposits occurring farther away from the escarpment must have moved much earlier because they have been smoothed by the action of glaciers and are capped by till. Although the Trotternish landslides are the most famous, there are others along the coast of northern Skye and in Glen Uig.

The survival of thick accumulations of weathered, frost-shattered rock on hilltops along the Trotternish Escarpment suggests that these summits, like those of the Cuillin, stood above the last ice sheet as 'nunataks', and so underwent no glacial scouring.

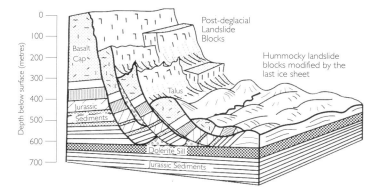

Reconstructed cross-section through the Storr landslides

Beaches

Modern beaches

Sandy beaches are not common on Skye because sandy sediment sources are scarce, the coast shelve too steeply, and wave energy is quickly dissipated along the long, deep sea lochs that are a feature of Skye's indented coastline. Most of the beaches are derived from glacial deposits; for example, many cobbles on the beach of Sleat have been carried from the mainland.

The dazzling creamy-white beaches known locally as coral sands are created by the calcareous alga *Lithothamnion*, which has a remarkable resemblance to branching coral and which flourishes in sheltered bays around the west coast. Broken fragments are continuously washed up and these unusual sands were used locally to 'lime' acid, peaty soils.

Ancient beaches and past changes of sea level

Benches and notches carved into the cliffs of northern and western Skye bear witness to relentless attrition by the sea over many thousands of years, adding to the splendour and mystery of this rugged coastline. These 'wave-cut platforms', some still capped by beach shingle, are a stark reminder that the sea was once as much as 30 metres higher than it is today. The platforms were created at various times over the past 500,000 years, during glacial periods when the earth's crust sagged under the enormous weight of ice sheets.

The 'Coral' Beach near Dunvegan Castle

During these periods the sea level rose in Scotland, even though the world's oceans were partly locked up in great continental ice sheets and sea level at the equator was actually 100 metres or more lower than today.

Two distinct sets of raised beaches occur on Skye. Those lying 15 to 30 metres above sea level formed as Scotland's last widespread ice sheet decayed, 14,000 to 13,000 years ago. A delta and raised beach that formed at this time provide a valuable source of sand and gravel near Kyleakin. The other set of raised beaches formed between 7,000 and 5,500 years ago during a period of rapid rise in world sea level caused by the melting of ice sheets in North America and Scandanavia and before Scotland had completely recovered from the unloading of its former ice cover. These raised beached occur up to 10 metres above present sea level; some are associated with long-abandonned caves, geos and sea stacks and at Braes, 12 kilometres south of Port Righ, the coast is linked to an island by an unusual gravel spit (a 'raised tombolo'). The raised beaches all tilt gently towards the west owing to varying uplift since deglaciation.

Lithothamnion calcareum

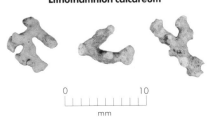

Scottish Natural Heritage
and the British Geological Survey

Scottish Natural Heritage is a government body. Its aim is to help people enjoy Scotland's natural heritage responsibly, understand it more fully and use it wisely so that it can be sustained for future generations.

Scottish Natural Heritage
12 Hope Terrace
Edinburgh EH9 2AS

**SCOTTISH
NATURAL
HERITAGE**

The British Geological Survey maintains up-to-date knowledge of the geology of the UK and its continental shelf. It carries out surveys and geological research.
The Scottish Office of BGS is sited in Edinburgh. The office runs an advisory and information service, a geological library and a well-stocked geological bookshop.

British Geological Survey
Murchison House, West Mains Road
Edinburgh EH9 3LA

**British
Geological Survey**
NATURAL ENVIRONMENTAL RESEARCH COUNCIL

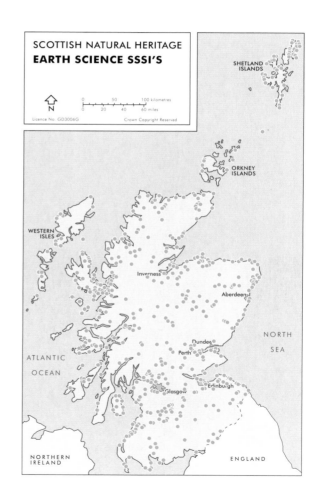

SCOTTISH NATURAL HERITAGE
EARTH SCIENCE SSSI'S

N

0   50   100 kilometres
0   20   40   60 miles

Licence No. GD3006G   Crown Copyright Reserved

SHETLAND ISLANDS

ORKNEY ISLANDS

WESTERN ISLES

Inverness

Aberdeen

ATLANTIC OCEAN

Dundee
Perth

NORTH SEA

Glasgow
Edinburgh

NORTHERN IRELAND

ENGLAND

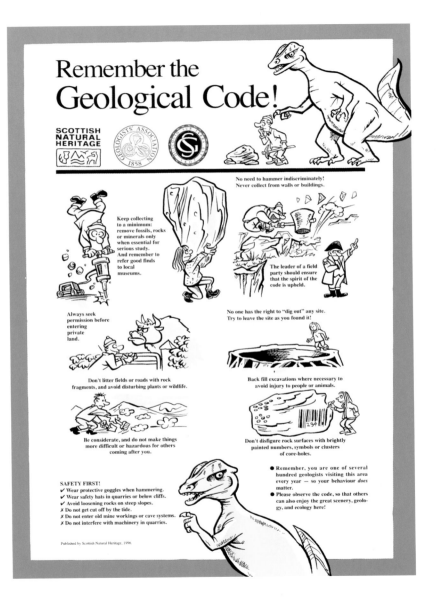

Remember the Geological Code!

SCOTTISH NATURAL HERITAGE

GEOLOGISTS ASSOCIATION 1858

Keep collecting to a minimum: remove fossils, rocks or minerals only when essential for serious study. And remember to refer good finds to local museums.

No need to hammer indiscriminately! Never collect from walls or buildings.

The leader of a field party should ensure that the spirit of the code is upheld.

Always seek permission before entering private land.

No one has the right to "dig out" any site. Try to leave the site as you found it!

Don't litter fields or roads with rock fragments, and avoid disturbing plants or wildlife.

Back fill excavations where necessary to avoid injury to people or animals.

Be considerate, and do not make things more difficult or hazardous for others coming after you.

Don't disfigure rock surfaces with brightly painted numbers, symbols or clusters of core-holes.

SAFETY FIRST!
✔ Wear protective goggles when hammering.
✔ Wear safety hats in quarries or below cliffs.
✔ Avoid loosening rocks on steep slopes.
✗ Do not get cut off by the tide.
✗ Do not enter old mine workings or cave systems.
✗ Do not interfere with machinery in quarries.

● Remember, you are one of several hundred geologists visiting this area every year — so your behaviour *does* matter.
● Please observe the code, so that others can also enjoy the great scenery, geology, and ecology here!

Published by Scottish Natural Heritage, 1996.

Also in the Landscape Fashioned by Geology series...

If you have enjoyed Skye why not find out more about the geology of some of Scotland's distinctive areas in our Landscape Fashioned by Geology series. Each book helps you to explore what lies beneath the soils, trees and heather with clear explanations, stunning photographs and illustrations. The series is produced in collaboration with the British Geological Society - written by experts in a style which is accessible to all.

Arran and the Clyde Islands

The diverse landscapes of Arran and the Clyde Islands mark the boundary between Highland and Lowland. Discover the ancient secrets and the appeal of these well-loved islands.
David McAdam & Steve Robertson
ISBN 1 85397 287 8 pbk 24pp £3.00

Cairngorms

Their broad plateaux, steep-sided glens and deep corries make the Cairngorms one of the foremost mountain landscapes in Britain. Discover how they were fashioned by weathering, glaciers and rivers.
John Gordon, Vanessa Brazier & Sarah Keast
ISBN 1 85397 086 7 pbk 28 pp £2.00

East Lothian and the Borders

Underneath the calm facade of south-east Scotland's fertile plains and rolling hills lies a complex structure, which reflects an eventful geological history.
David McAdam & Phil Stone
ISBN 1 85397 242 8 pbk 26pp £3.00

Edinburgh

Some of the most important discoveries in geological science were made in and around Edinburgh. This booklet is full of startling facts about the Capital's geological past.
David McAdam
ISBN 1 85397 024 7 pbk 28pp £2.50

Loch Lomond to Stirling

The heart of Scotland, from the low carse to the mountain tops, encompasses some of the most diverse landscapes in Scotland. Find out how these modern landscapes reflect the geological changes of the past.
Mike Browne & John Mendum
ISBN 1 85397 119 7 pbk 26pp £2.00

Orkney and Shetland

These northern outposts of Scotland hold a great fascination for the geologist. Starting 3 billion years ago their story tells of colliding continents, bizarre lifeforms and a landscape which continues to be eroded by the pounding force of the Atlantic.
Clive Auton, Terry Fletcher & David Gould
ISBN 1 85397 220 7 pbk 24pp £2.50

Scotland: the creation of its natural landscape

Scotland: the Creation of its Natural Landscape provides a wealth of information on how Scotland was created and the events that took place there through the aeons. But the story doesn't stop back in the mists of time, it continually unfolds and this book provides up to the minute information on geological events taking place beneath our feet. It also provides a history of geological science and highlights the enormous contribution Scots geologists have made to the world.
Alan McKirdy and Roger Crofts
ISBN 1 85397 004 2 pbk 64pp £7.50

Series Editor: Alan McKirdy (SNH)

SNH Publications Order Form

Title	Price	Quantity
Arran & the Clyde Islands	£3.00	
Cairngorms	£2.00	
East Lothian & the Borders	£3.00	
Edinburgh	£2.50	
Loch Lomond to Stirling	£2.00	
Orkney & Shetland	£2.50	
Scotland: the creation of its natural landscape	£7.50	
Skye	£3.95	

Postage and packaging: free of charge within the UK

Please complete in BLOCK CAPITALS

Name _____

Address _____

_____

_____

Post Code

Type of Credit Card   VISA ☐   MasterCard ☐

Name of card holder _____

Card Number ☐☐☐☐ ☐☐☐☐ ☐☐☐☐ ☐☐☐☐

Expiry Date ☐☐ ☐☐

Send order and cheque made payable to Scottish Natural Heritage to:

Scottish Natural Heritage, Design and Publications, Battleby, Redgorton, Perth PH1 3EW

E-mail: pubs@redgore.demon.co.uk   www.snh.org.uk

Please add my name to the mailing list for the: SNH Magazine ☐

Publications Catalogue ☐